T0163781

GUERRILLA
MARKETING
FOR THE NEW
MILLENNIUM

LESSONS FROM THE
FATHER OF
GUERRILLA MARKETING

JAY CONRAD LEVINSON
BEST SELLING AUTHOR WITH OVER 14 MILLION BOOKS SOLD

GUERRILLA MARKETING FOR THE NEW MILLENNIUM

By Jay Conrad Levinson

© 2005 Jay Conrad Levinson and Guerrilla Marketing International. All rights reserved.

ISBN: 1-933596-07-4   Paperback

ISBN: 1-933596-08-2   e-Book

ISBN: 1-933596-09-0   Audio

Published by:

MORGAN · JAMES
PUBLISHING FOR THE REST OF US...

Morgan James Publishing, LLC
1225 Franklin Ave Ste 325
Garden City, NY 11530-1693
Toll Free 800-485-4943
www.MorganJamesPublishing.com

Cover and Inside Design by:
Heather Kirk
www.GraphicsByHeather.com
Heather@GraphicsByHeather.com

Habitat for Humanity®
Peninsula
Building Partner

CRITICS ARE RAVING

"Your guerrilla marketing talk was definitely the highlight of our seminar schedule. In fact, many veteran attendees proclaimed you as the best speaker we have presented in our eight-year history."

~ David Scroggy, Director, Comic Book Expo

"A source of inspiration for many independent entrepreneurs."

~ Booklist

"Every book by Jay Levinson is worth reading."

~ Jane Applegate, author of Succeeding in Small Business

"Slam dunk! Without exception, every person who attended our guerrilla marketing seminar said it was well worth their time. Some even commented that they were glad others did not show up because now they have a jump on their competition."

~ Julie Lopresti, Advertising Manager, Pacific Bell

"Ask almost any successful entrepreneur what the best book is for building a small business, and one of Levinson's titles will surely come up."

~ Entrepreneur Business Success Guide

"You gave us concise, practical ideas to implement directly, and virtually all of them were applicable and affordable. Our franchisers are now

committed guerrillas and they will need what is really marketing weapon number one, a book full of more of your terrific ideas. You are, by far, the best and more popular speaker we have ever had and PostalAnnex+ is sure to benefit from your presentation for years to come."

~ David Wilkey, Director of Marketing, PostalAnnex+

"After 'Guerrilla Marketing' became a best-seller, the series took on a life of its own....irrevocably tied in with the unconventional, non-textbook, and practical wisdom of guerrilla business practices for small business."

~ Home Office Computing

"A veritable plum pudding of marketing techniques and secrets."

~ Los Angeles Times

"'Wow!' is the first word that comes to mind when I think of your presentation at Entrepreneur's Day. You really gave our attendees some great advice and tactics to market their businesses more effectively and aggressively."

~ Melissa Anderson, Manager, Public Relations;
The Enterprise Corporation of Pittsburgh

"We can fully appreciate the value of your condensation of marketing techniques into a simple to use format."

~ Jerald N. Cohn, PakMail Centers of America

"Jay did a super job here in Denver. The Guerrilla Marketing Weapons Workshop was a great success, as was his talk at lunch. I heard from many of the attendees that the event was well worth the time and money spent."

~ Joyce Schlose, Manager, The Small Business Profit Center, Greater Denver Chamber of Commerce

"Dear Jay — the recent Business Solutions Forum was a huge success. Key to its success was the high quality of the keynote presentations — these presentations set the bar very high and created the right environment for the AT&T case studies that followed. In fact, one of the keynote presentations remains the subject of a great deal of conversation today. I guess it was simply delivered better and had more real content. It was yours....we thank you!"

~ Macy Jones, Director of Development, Strategic Marketing, Inc.

"Thank you for being part of INTEC's Annual Marketing Meeting last week. Your presentation was outstanding. We heard nothing but positive comments from our members."

~ Dennis C. Hardy, President, INTEC & Company, Inc.

"Thank you for the presentation 'Guerrilla Marketing for Your Small and Growing Business.' Our audience enjoyed it very much. Your contribution to the Quality Learning Series is greatly appreciated."

~ Lisa M. Finley, Marketing Coordinator, U.S. Chamber of Commerce

"Your keynote presentation was terrific. The NBIA Board, staff and audience very much enjoyed your presentation."

~ Dinah Adkins, Executive Director,
National Business Incubation Association

"Your speech at Entrepreneur's Day was great! What a good way to kick-off this conference with such a strong emphasis on marketing. Guerrilla Marketing is just what these entrepreneurs need to understand. Your style and delivery was excellent and I heard many young entrepreneurs talk about the impact it made."

~ John R. Thorne, Chairman, Carnegie Mellon

"We had well over 140 people attend the event and every single one I spoke with was pleased at the value they received and were excited about applying the concepts that you presented to them. You may be interested to know that our chamber will soon be designating its own 'guerrilla marketer' to help promote our services and programs.

~ Ben Buehler-Garcia, Group Vice President,
Tucson Metropolitan Chamber of Commerce

"We have received a great deal of positive feedback and by all standards the Conference was an overwhelming hit — the best one yet! We congratulate you on your outstanding performance that contributed to the Conference's success."

~ Lisa Schaertl and Scott Rothchild,
The Annual Catalog Conference and Exhibition

"Your comments set the stage for a healthy debate about the difficult challenges of achieving future success in an industry historically supported by tremendous asset growth and strong capital markets."

~ Gregory T. Rogers, President, FutureWatch

"The pens and pencils were definitely flying during your presentation of 100 guerrilla marketing tips. Over 85% of survey respondents gave your presentation high ratings. The others, I am sure, simply had a hard time keeping up with your rapid-fire tips, tactics and suggestions."

~ William Annesley, Chief Marketing Officer,
Invisible Fence Company

"The seminar was a huge success. I have received nothing but positive comments about his presentation. We had a great time."

~ Gary Nicholds, Williamson Medical Center

"Your presentation was absolutely fantastic and the feedback has been quite positive."

~ Karlene Johnson, Managing Director, Johnson Communications

The content was great, and I believe that most of our members either heard new material or were given the opportunity to reexamine forgotten concepts. On the whole, I would rate your presentation highly."

~ Eric J. Newman, President, North Bay
Association for Mortgage Brokers

"Your presence certainly helped to make the day a success. Your discussion of guerrilla marketing weapons and methods was pertinent to the issues facing today's business people. Our exit survey results reflected the praise I heard from many of the attendees. The audience reaction to your speech was excellent and many commented on how refreshing it was to receive not only philosophy on how to run a business, but the tools and methods they can implement immediately to see results."

~ Suzanne Clements, Retail Products Manager, The Wichita Eagle

"Marketing whiz wows area CEOs. Jay Levinson, customer analyst and author of widely published books on 'guerrilla marketing,' won over 70 Atlanta-area chief executives Tuesday. He told them how to win over customers."

~ Susan Harte, The Atlanta Journal

"Jay, thank you for your continued contribution to small biz. You are a joy to work with and I couldn't imagine the site without you."

~ Kathleen Doll, Microsoft Small Biz Website Manager

"Jay, as one who has, if not made a living, at least made some money, out of writing, I have the greatest admiration for you, not just for who and what you are, but how cogently you have been able to put your great marketing ideas into such excellently received books."

~ Gerardo Joffe, Author and successful entrepreneur

WE BEGIN WITH A BIO OF JAY CONRAD LEVINSON

Jay Conrad Levinson is the author of the best-selling marketing series in history, "*Guerrilla Marketing*," plus 27 other business books. His guerrilla concepts have influenced marketing so much that today his books appear in 41 languages and are required reading in many MBA programs worldwide.

Jay taught guerrilla marketing for ten years at the extension division of the University of California in Berkeley. And he was a practitioner of it in the United States — as Senior Vice-President at J. Walter Thompson, and in Europe, as Creative Director and Board Member at Leo Burnett Advertising.

He has written a monthly column for *Entrepreneur Magazine*, articles for *Inc. Magazine*, and writes online columns published monthly on the Microsoft Website — in addition to occasional columns in the *San Francisco Examiner*. He also writes online columns regularly for Onvia.com, FreeAgent.com and MarketMakers.com, and InfoUsa.com in addition to occasional columns for Guru.com.

Jay is the Chairman of Guerrilla Marketing International, a marketing partner of Adobe and Apple. He has served on the Microsoft Small Business Council and the 3Com Small Business Advisory Board.

His *Guerrilla Marketing* is a series of books, audio tapes, video-tapes, an award-winning CD-ROM, a newsletter, a consulting organization, an Internet website, and a way for you to spend less, get more, and achieve substantial profits.

TABLE OF CONTENTS

CHAPTER 1

What Is Guerrilla Marketing?

WHAT IS GUERRILLA MARKETING?

Guerrilla Marketing is unconventional strategies, secrets, and tactics for earning conventional goals — big profits from your small business.

~By Jay Conrad Levinson

This guerrilla marketing course will explore the 16 guerrilla marketing concepts that guarantee success, the 100 guerrilla marketing weapons, the structure for a seven-sentence guerrilla marketing strategy and the ten steps you must take to succeed at a guerrilla marketing attack.

Along with these concepts, the course will provide a flowing river of information that can make your marketing investment pay off handsomely while preventing you from wasting one cent of your precious marketing budget.

If you are interested in generating profits for your small business, medium business, huge business, or professional practice, this is the right place for you to be looking. I intend to give you valuable information that can contribute mightily to the profitability of your enterprise. I view this opportunity to enrich your coffers as a course for guerrillas. If you take marketing and profitability seriously, you'll consult this book regularly, and your new guerrilla insights will soon be apparent on your profit and loss statement. Let's go!

WHAT IS MARKETING IN THE FIRST PLACE?

Marketing is absolutely every bit of contact any part of your business has with any segment of the public. Guerrillas view marketing as a circle that begins with your ideas for generating revenue and continues on with the goal of amassing a large number of repeat and referral customers.

The three keys words in that paragraph are EVERY, REPEAT, and REFERRAL. If your marketing is not a circle, it's a straight line that leads directly into Chapters 7, 11, or 13 in the bankruptcy courts.

HOW IS GUERRILLA MARKETING DIFFERENT FROM TRADITIONAL MARKETING?

Guerrilla marketing means marketing that is unconventional, non-traditional, not by-the-book, and extremely flexible. Twenty factors make it different from old-fashioned marketing:

1. Instead of investing money in the marketing process, you invest time, energy, imagination, and information.

2. Instead of using guesswork in your marketing, you use the science of psychology, actual laws of human behavior.

3. Instead of concentrating on traffic, responses, or gross sales, profits are the only yardstick by which you measure your marketing.

4. Instead of being oriented to companies with limitless bank accounts, guerrilla marketing is geared to small business.

5. Instead of ignoring customers once they've purchased, you have a fervent devotion to customer follow-up.

6. Instead of intimidating small business owners, guerrilla marketing removes the mystique from the entire marketing process, clarifies it.

7. Instead of competing with other businesses, guerrilla marketing preaches the gospel of cooperation, urging you to help others and let them help you.

8. Instead of trying to make sales, guerrillas are dedicated to making relationships, for long-term relationships are paramount in the new millennium.

9. Instead of believing that single marketing weapons such as advertising or a website work, guerrillas know that only marketing combinations work.

10. Instead of encouraging you to advertise, guerrilla marketing provides you with 100 different marketing weapons; advertising is only one of them.

11. Instead of growing large and diversifying, guerrillas grow profitably and then maintain their focus — not an easy thing to do.

12. Instead of aiming messages at large groups, guerrilla marketing is aimed at individuals and small groups.

13. Instead of being unintentional by identifying only mass marketing, guerrilla marketing is always intentional, embracing even such details as how your telephone is answered.

14. Instead of growing linearly by adding new customers, guerrillas grow geometrically by enlarging the size of each transaction, generating more repeat sales, leaning upon the enormous referral power of customers, and adding new customers.

15. Instead of thinking of what a business can take, guerrilla marketing asks that you think of what a business can give — in the way of free information to help customers and prospects.

16. Instead of ignoring technology in marketing, guerrilla marketing encourages you to be techno-cozy and if you're techno-phobia, advises you to see a techno-shrink because techno-phobia is fatal these days.

17. Instead of being me marketing and talking about a business, guerrilla marketing is you marketing and talks about the prospect.

18. Instead of attempting to make a sale with marketing, guerrilla marketing attempts to gain consent with marketing, then uses that consent to market only to interested people.

19. Instead of being a monolog with one person doing all the talking, guerrilla marketing is a dialog with interactivity.

20. Instead of limiting you to a handful of marketing weapons, guerrilla marketing provides you with 100 marketing weapons, and 62 of those are free.

These are very critical differences and are probably the reasons that the concept of guerrilla marketing has filled a void in the world's economy, explaining why the guerrilla marketing books have been translated into 41 languages, sold over 14 million copies, are required reading in most MBA programs, are available in audio tape and videotape versions, as computer software, as a nationally-syndicated column, as a newsletter, as an interactive association, and are the most popular and widely-read marketing books in the world.

GUERRILLA EXERCISE:

Compare your marketing with the 20 ways Guerrilla Marketing is different to see how many differences you already embrace. Your goal is to run your business by all 20.

Put a checkmark next to each difference your company puts into action:

1. _____   I invest time, energy and imagination rather than only money.

2. _____   My marketing is based upon psychology more than guesswork.

3. _____   I measure my marketing performance by profits more than any other yardstick.

4. _____   I embrace the principles of small business marketing more than large business marketing.

5. _____   I follow-up all sales with customer contact and never ignore customers after they have purchased.

6. _____   I am not intimidated by the marketing process and feel in control of my marketing.

7. _____   My radar is attuned to cooperation in a quest to partner with others in co-marketing programs.

8. _____ I tally up new relationships my company has made at the end of each month.

9. _____ I employ combinations of marketing weapons rather than relying on only one.

10. _____ I utilize a wide assortment of marketing weapons in the attainment of my business goals.

11. _____ I am able to focus upon the main thrust of my business rather than looking for ways to diversify.

12. _____ I direct my marketing to individuals and small groups more than large groups of people.

13. _____ All of my marketing is intentional; I know marketing is any contact between my company and anyone else.

14. _____ I strive to grow my company geometrically rather than linearly.

15. _____ I freely give things away that can help my customers and prospects attain their own goals.

16. _____ I use technology to strengthen my marketing and I have no fear of using it.

17. _____ My marketing messages are stated from my prospects' and customers' points of view rather than my own.

18. _____ My marketing attempts to gain consent from people to continue receiving my marketing materials.

19. _____ I am certain to make my marketing a dialog and always elicit feedback.

20. _____ I am using a wide variety of guerilla marketing weapons.

GUERRILLA ACTION STEPS:

A. Review where you put checkmarks on the checklist above and circle the numbers at which no checkmark appears. These are the areas that need altering in your method of marketing.

B. Decide upon the specific actions that you will take for each statement so as to polish and perfect the performance of your marketing by transforming it into pure Guerrilla Marketing. List these in the space provided beneath each statement for which you have circled the number.

C. Take the actions you have listed, one by one, until each of the statements merits a checkmark. Your goal is a checkmark by each statement.

CHAPTER 2

The New Secrets Of Guerrilla Marketing

THE NEW SECRETS OF GUERRILLA MARKETING

If you memorize these 16 words and run your business by the concepts they represent, you will exceed your most optimistic goals.

~By Jay Conrad Levinson

The most important things you need to know about marketing are in this chapter. In the few minutes it takes you to read this, you'll learn more basic truths about marketing than you'd pick up with a score of MBA degrees under one arm and all the marketing books ever written, including mine, under the other.

As marketing continues to change, the secrets of guerrilla marketing continue to change. Originally, there were three secrets, then seven, then twelve. Now, I'm going to clue you in on the 16 secrets that guarantee you will exceed your most hopeful projections, however dreamy they may be.

MEMORIZE THESE 16 WORDS THEN LIVE BY THEM.

I'm giving you a memory crutch so that you'll never forget these words, each one representing a major guerrilla marketing secret. All 16 words end in the letters "ENT." Run your business by the guerrilla concepts they represent and your marketing dreams will come true.

1. **COMMITMENT**: You should know that a mediocre marketing program with commitment will always prove more profitable than a brilliant marketing program without commitment. Commitment makes it happen.

2. **INVESTMENT**: Marketing is not an expense, but an investment — the best investment available in America today — if you do it right. With the 16 secrets of guerrilla marketing to guide you, you'll be doing it right.

3. **CONSISTENT**: It takes a while for prospects to trust you and if you change your marketing, media, and identity, you're hard to trust. Restraint is a great ally of the guerrilla. Repetition is another.

4. **CONFIDENT**: In a nationwide test to determine why people buy, price came in fifth, selection fourth, service third, quality second, and, in first place — people said they patronize businesses in which they are confident.

5. **PATIENT**: Unless the person running your marketing is patient, it will be difficult to practice commitment, view marketing as an investment, be consistent, and make prospects confident. Patience is a guerrilla virtue.

6. **ASSORTMENT**: Guerrillas know that individual marketing weapons rarely work on their own. But marketing combinations do work. A wide assortment of marketing tools is required to woo and win customers.

7. **CONVENIENT**: People now know that time is not money, but is far more valuable than money. Respect this by being easy to do business with and running your company for the convenience of your customers, not yourself.

8. **SUBSEQUENT**: The real profits come after you've made the sale, in the form of repeat and referral business. Non-guerrillas think marketing ends when they've made the sale. Guerrillas know that's when marketing begins.

9. **AMAZEMENT**: There are elements of your business that you take for granted, but prospects would be amazed if they knew the details. Be sure all of your marketing always reflects that amazement. It's always there.

10. **MEASUREMENT**: You can actually double your profits by measuring the results of your marketing. Some weapons hit bulls-eyes. Others miss the target. Unless you measure, you won't know which is which.

11. **INVOLVEMENT**: This describes the relationship between you and your customers — and it is a relationship. You prove

your involvement by following up; they prove theirs by patronizing and recommending you.

12. **DEPENDENT**: The guerrilla's job is not to compete but to cooperate with other businesses. Market them in return for them marketing you. Set up tie-ins with others. Become dependent to market more and invest less.

13. **ARMAMENT**: Armament is defined as "the equipment necessary to wage and win battles." The armament of guerrillas is technology: computers, current software, cell phones, pagers, fax machines, wireless communications.

14. **CONSENT**: In an era of non-stop interruption marketing, the key to success is to first gain consent to receive your marketing materials, then market only to those who have given you that consent. Don't waste money on people who don't give it to you.

15. **AUGMENT**: To succeed online, augment your website with offline promotion, constant maintenance of your site, participation in newsgroups and forums, email, chatroom attendance, posting articles, hosting conferences and rapid follow-up.

16. **CONTENT**: Marketing is information that can benefit the lives of those to whom it is aimed, the truth made fasci-

nating. If your marketing lives up to that definition, it has to be rich in content.

These 16 concepts are probably the reason that many start-up guerrillas now run highly successful companies. They are the cornerstone of guerrilla marketing. Just 16 words, but each one nuclear-powered and capable of propelling you into the land of your dreams.

GUERRILLA EXERCISE:

Measure your own company by how many of these concepts dictate your marketing. Compare them, one by one, with the way you currently run your marketing program. The idea is to run it by all 16.

Put a checkmark next to each of the guerrilla principles that you understand and embrace to run the marketing of your business:

_____ Commitment

_____ Investment

_____ Consistent

_____ Confident

_____ Patient

_____ Assortment

_____ Convenient

_____ Subsequent

_____ Amazement

_____ Measurement

_____ Involvement

_____ Dependent

_____ Armament

_____ Consent

_____ Augment

_____ Content

GUERRILLA ACTION STEPS:

A. Review where you put checkmarks on the checklist above and circle the words at which no checkmark appears. These are the areas that need altering in your method of marketing.

B. Decide upon the specific actions that you will take for each "ent" concept so you can capitalize upon each secret of Guerrilla Marketing. List these in the space provided beneath each of the 16 concepts.

C. Take the actions you have listed, one by one, until each of the concepts merits a checkmark. Your goal is a checkmark by each concept.

CHAPTER 3

Guerrilla Marketing Weapons

GUERRILLA MARKETING WEAPONS

Your marketing arsenal can be much more potent than it is right now, and it won't even require much of an investment.

~By Jay Conrad Levinson

Ask the average business owner what marketing is and you'll be told that it's advertising. Guerrillas know that this is nonsense. Advertising is only one weapon of marketing. How many weapons are most business owners aware of? Maybe five or ten. How many do they use? Possibly three. But *guerrillas are aware of a full 100 guerrilla marketing weapons* and make use of about 40 of them. More than half of the weapons are free! Here, because this course wants you to be as lethal as possible, are ALL 100 weapons.

I present them in no particular rank or order because there's a 100-way tie for first place. Still, you will come across a few weapons that deserve red neon asterisks inside your head. Your job now as a business owner is to do what you can to use as many weapons as possible. Okay?

1. Marketing plan

2. Marketing calendar

3. Niche/Positioning

4. Name of company

5. Identity

6. Logo

7. Theme

8. Stationary

9. Business card

10. Inside signs

11. Outside signs

12. Hours of operation

13. Days of operation

14. Package and label

15. Flexibility

16. Word-of-mouth

17. Community involvement

18. Neatness

19. Referral program

20. Sharing with others

21. Guarantee or warranty

22. Telemarketing scripts

23. Gift certificates

24. Printed brochures

25. Electronic brochures

26. Location

27. Advertising

28. Sales training

29. Networking

30. Quality

31. Reprints and blow-ups

32. Flip charts

33. Opportunities to upgrade

34. Contests/sweepstakes

35. Barter options

36. Club memberships

37. Partial payment plans

38. Phone demeanor

39. Toll-free phone number

40. Cause (environment)

41. Free consultations

42. Free seminars

43. Free demos or tours

44. Free samples

45. Giver vs taker stance

46. Fusion marketing

47. Marketing on hold

48. Past success stories

49. Attire

50. Service

51. Follow-up

52. Yourself and your employees

53. Free gifts

54. Catalog

55. Yellow pages ad

56. Column in a publication

57. Article in a publication

58. Speaker at a club

59. Newsletter

60. All your audiences

61. Benefits of your offering

62. Computer

63. Selection

64. Contact time with customers

65. How you say hello and goodbye

66. Public relations

67. Publicity contacts

68. Online marketing

69. Classified ads

70. Newspaper ads

71. Magazine ads

72. Radio commercials

73. TV spots

74. Infomercials

75. Movie commercials

76. Direct mail letters

77. Direct mail postcards

78. Postcard for postcard deck

79. Outdoor billboards

80. Fax-on-demand

81. Special events

82. Show displays and staff

83. Audio-visual aids

84. Posters

85. Prospect mailing lists

86. Research studies

87. Competitive advantages

88. Marketing insight

89. Speed

90. Testimonials

91. Reputation

92. Enthusiasm

93. Credibility

94. Spying on self and others

95. Easy to do business with

96. Brand name awareness

97. Designated guerrilla

98.   Customer mailing list

99.   Competitiveness

100. Satisfied customers

These 100 weapons should be considered for every guerrilla's arsenal. Once you've selected them: put them into priority order, set a date for the launching of the weapon, and appoint a person to mastermind your use of the weapons you've selected. Whatever you do, launch your guerrilla marketing attack IN SLOW MOTION, only launching weapons when you can utilize them properly at a pace that is comfortable emotionally and financially. After launching, KEEP TRACK because some weapons will hit bull's-eyes while others will miss the target. Unless you keep track, you won't know which is which. Guerrillas always know which is which.

GUERRILLA EXERCISE:

Review each weapon and place it into one of four categories: Using Properly Now, Using But Needs Improvement, Not Using But Should, Not Appropriate Now. Your job is to work at your marketing so as to make the first category as lengthy as possible and to eliminate the second and third categories completely.

Total the number of weapons in each category:

_____ Weapons I use properly now

_____ Weapons that need improvement

_____ Weapons I don't use, but should

_____ Weapons not appropriate right now

____**100**____ The total of all four categories

GUERRILLA ACTION STEPS:

A. List the weapons that need improvement.

B. Make the improvement in your use of each of those weapons.

C. List the weapons you don't use, but should.

D. Launch each weapon you deem appropriate for your business at this time.

You need not utilize all 100 weapons, but you do need to improve the weapons requiring improvement, and you should be using all the weapons you believe can help increase your profits.

CHAPTER 4

Guerrilla Marketing Strategy

GUERRILLA MARKETING STRATEGY

Running a business without a marketing strategy is like driving into a new nation without a road map to guide you.

~By Jay Conrad Levinson

I am flabbergasted that so many businesses operate without a marketing strategy. It's like entering battle under a commander who orders you: READY! FIRE! AIM! A guerrilla marketing strategy prevents hit and miss marketing and enables you to hit the bull's-eye of your target with every single shot you take.

A guerrilla marketing strategy has only seven sentences. It is brief because of two important reasons. Number one, a seven-sentence strategy forces you to focus, and number two, everyone in your organization can read and understand a simple seven-sentence marketing strategy, putting them smack dab on your wave length. Proctor and Gamble may be the most sophisticated marketing company on the planet. All their brands are guided by brief, seven-sentence strategies.

They may have 50 more pages of documentation, but the focus is winnowed down to seven sentences. And only one of them has to be a long sentence.

Let's say you run a service that teaches people how to operate computers. Let's say the name of your company is Computer Tutor. And finally, let's say you have the mind and goals of a guerrilla. Here's how a guerrilla marketing strategy would work for you.

1. The first sentence tells the purpose of your marketing.

   The purpose of Computer Tutor marketing is to book 100% of the company's available time for computer education at the lowest possible cost per hour.

2. The second sentence tells how you'll achieve your purpose, concentrating upon your benefits and your competitive advantage or advantages.

   This will be accomplished by establishing the credentials of the educators, the location of the operation, and the training equipment.

3. The third sentence tells your target audience — or audiences.

   Our target market is local small business owners who can benefit from learning to operate a computer; our secondary market is large corporations.

4. The fourth sentence tells the marketing weapons you'll use.

   Marketing weapons to be utilized will be a combination of personal letters, circulars, brochures, signs on bulletin boards, classified ads in local newspapers, yellow pages advertising, direct mail special offers, advertising specialties, free seminars, sampling, a referral program, telephone training, professional office decor and employee attire, a website offering a free newsletter, and publicity in the local newspapers, on radio talk shows, and on television.

5. The fifth sentence tells your niche in the market.

We will position ourselves as the prime source of one-on-one, guaranteed instruction in the operation of small computers.

6. The sixth sentence tells your identity.

Our identity will be a blend of professionalism, personal attention, and warm human regard for our students, and the role of computers in their lives and their businesses.

7. The seventh sentence tells your marketing budget as a percent of your projected gross sales. (In 1999, the average U.S. business invested 4 percent.)

Ten percent of projected gross sales will be allocated to marketing.

This strategy should guide your efforts for the next one to fifty years. Use it to measure ALL marketing materials you plan to use.

No matter how much you may love them, if they do not fulfill your strategy, toss them right into your wastebasket.

You should review your guerrilla marketing annually and make slight tweaks in it, especially in the fourth sentence, but the idea is to get it right the first time, then commit to it — making sure all your employees and co-workers read it and know what you're up to. You'll be up to earning record-breaking profits, and the bright light of your guerrilla marketing strategy will illuminate your path.

GUERRILLA EXERCISE:

Write a seven-sentence guerrilla marketing strategy for your business. Follow the format I've just described, then pin the written strategy up inside your head.

1. The purpose of my marketing is:

_____

_____

_____

2. I will accomplish this purpose by stressing my:

_____

_____

_____

3. My target audience or audiences is:

_____

_____

_____

4. Marketing weapons I plan to employ are:

_____

_____

_____

_____

_____

5. My niche in the marketplace is:

_____

_____

_____

6. My business identity is:

_____

_____

_____

7. I plan to devote _____ percent of gross sales to marketing.

GUERRILLA ACTION STEPS:

A. Show your completed marketing plan to everyone in your organization who is involved with marketing.

B. Show your completed marketing plan to each of your employees, even if they are not involved with your marketing.

C. Breathe life into your plan by doing exactly what you say you will do and measuring all your marketing materials, current and future, against the strategy. If they do not follow the strategy, change them or discard them.

CHAPTER 5

Guerrilla Marketing Personality Traits

GUERRILLA MARKETING PERSONALITY TRAITS

Guerrilla Marketers are both born guerrillas and made guerrillas. If they lack these traits, they work to develop them.

~By Jay Conrad Levinson

While working with the marketing honchos of Fortune 500 companies and the marketing chiefs of new up-and-coming companies that want like crazy to be members of the Fortune 500, I've noticed eight personality traits that these marketing geniuses possessed. And try as I may, I simply have not found an exception to this guerrilla observation. People who run successful marketing departments have every one of these eight characteristics.

I hope that you already have all eight of these personality traits, or that you can at least develop the one or two that may be lacking. Otherwise, I urge you to turn the task of marketing over to somebody else because marketing is going to get you in trouble and the way you use marketing will get your company in trouble. Let's examine the eight right here and right now:

1. **PATIENCE:** I start with this trait because it's the most important by far. A study was conducted to see how many times you must penetrate a person's mind with your selling

proposition before you convert that person from a state of total apathy to a state of purchase readiness. Amazingly, the researchers came up with an answer. It was nine. Your message must penetrate a mind nine times before that person will buy what you are selling. And that's the good news. The bad news is that for every three times you put out the word, your prospects are paying attention only one time.

So you market by advertising, emailing, telemarketing, signs, direct mail, anything — and you put the word out three times and it penetrates your prospect's mind one time. What do you suppose happens? Nothing happens. Zilch. Okay, you put the word out six times, entering the mind of your prospect two times. What happens then?

Again, not one thing happens. All right, now you put the word out nine times and you have penetrated the mind of your prospect three times. What happens?

Your prospect knows he or she has heard of you before. That's what happens. No sale. No cigar. Not yet at least.

Sticking with the drill, you put out the word twelve times and your prospect's mind has been pierced four times. What happens then? What happens is that your prospect realizes he or she has seen your marketing before and people figure that if they keep seeing your marketing, you must be doing something right. But still, nobody is buying anything.

Now, you put out the word 15 times and penetrate your prospect's mind five times. At this point, the prospect probably reads every word of your ad or letter, probably even sends away for the brochure you've been offering all along. At this point, most small advertisers figure they've been doing everything wrong and so they abandon their marketing program. DON'T DO IT! NOT YET! This horrid state of affairs is called sellus interruptus. The sale is never consummated because the marketing chief didn't have the patience to hang in there.

After you've put the word out 18 times, and you've penetrated a mind six times, the person begins to think of when they'll make the purchase. Put out the word 21 times and you've penetrated a mind seven times. The person begins to think of where they'll get the money, how they'll pay. Put out the word 24 times and the prospects, with their minds penetrated eight times, write in their datebook when they will buy from you. They check with whoever they must check with before making a purchase. Finally, you get the word out 27 times, penetrate your prospects' minds nine times, then they buy from you. Eventually, the profits come rolling in.

Think that process can take place if you have no patience? NO WAY. That's why patience remains the most important of the eight personality characteristics.

2. **IMAGINATION**: This doesn't necessarily refer to headlines or graphics or jingles or being clever as much as it does facing

up to reality. If you're going to do a direct mailing, face up to the fact that everyone and their cousin does direct mailings. Why should your envelope get opened?

Because you've got the imagination to pop for first class postage and to put multiple stamps on your envelope – a combination of 6-centers, 3-centers, and 2-centers to add up to the current cost of postage at the time you are doing your mailing. Who could resist opening an envelope with so many stamps? Not only will it be opened, but it will be opened first. Doesn't take a lot of money, does takes a powerful imagination.

3. **SENSITIVITY**: People who run first-rate marketing shows are sensitive to their market, their prospects, the economy, the community, and the competition. It's a key personality trait.

4. **EGO STRENGTH**: The first people who will tire of your marketing program will be your co-workers, followed closely by your employees, your family, and your friends. They will counsel you to change because they are bored.

    Your prospects are not bored and have barely heard of you. Your customers will not be bored and will forever read your marketing materials to justify the fact that they still do business with you.

5. **AGGRESSIVENESS**: You need to be aggressive in your spending and thinking. When you hear that the average U.S. business

invested 4 percent of gross revenues in marketing in 2004, you want to invest 6 percent, 10 percent. When you hear there are 100 marketing weapons, you want to use at least half of them.

6. **CONSTANT LEARNING**: A seagull flies in endless circles, seeking food. When it finds food, it eats its fill, then flies in circles again, looking for more food. Seagulls just have to look for food. Humans have one instinct that is just as strong. Know what it is? To learn. Successful guerrillas know a lot, but keep learning more.

7. **GENEROSITY**: Guerrillas view marketing as an opportunity to help their prospects and customers succeed at their goals, whatever they may be. They think of things they can give away to help those people. They are generous with their time and their information.

8. **TAKE ACTION**: Many people read books, hear tapes, take courses and attend seminars. But most of them keep this information within them. Guerrillas learn the very same ways, but take action based upon what they have learned. They know that action is the power behind guerrilla marketing.

Those are the eight and the only eight traits that great marketing directors seem to have in common. I sure hope all eight words apply to you.

GUERRILLA EXERCISE:

Benjamin Franklin said that the three hardest things in the world are diamonds, steel and knowing yourself. Compare the eight guerrilla personality traits with your own, then be honest in knowing which ones you must develop even more.

Put a checkmark next to each of the guerrilla marketing personality characteristics that you possess. The character traits that I currently have are:

_____ Patience

_____ Imagination

_____ Sensitivity

_____ Ego strength

_____ Aggressiveness

_____ Constant learning

_____ Generosity

_____ Take action

GUERRILLA ACTION STEPS:

A. Circle each personality trait that does not have a checkmark.

B. Begin developing those traits in yourself.

C. Put a checkmark next to each trait that you are able to develop. The goal is to have a checkmark next to each trait.

CHAPTER 6

The Guerrilla
Marketing Attack

THE GUERRILLA MARKETING ATTACK

Mounting a Guerrilla Marketing attack is a process that begins with the easy parts, then asks more of you as the attack gains momentum.

~By Jay Conrad Levinson

Succeeding with a guerrilla marketing attack is a ten step process. Take all ten steps and watch your profits rise and your competitors cringe.

It's not as hard as you may think to succeed at a guerrilla marketing attack. And if you launch one properly, you'll find that succeeding at business is also not as hard as you may have thought. Don't even think of skipping any of the ten steps to success because all ten are necessary. We're not talking about playing with marketing. We're talking about succeeding with marketing.

1. The first step is to research everything you can. That means carefully investigating your market, your product or service, your competition, your industry and your options in media. It means looking into the benefits you offer, into the latest technology and into the makeup of your existing customers.

What media reaches your target audience? What media makes them respond and buy? Should you focus on advertising or direct marketing or a combination of the two? Do you need a website and if so, why?

There are answers to these questions and guerrillas have the knack for coming up with the right answers. As a person who is already connected to the Internet, you've got a head start in the research department. There is loads of information online that can propel you in the direction of success.

2. The second step is to write a benefits list. Have a meeting. Invite your key personnel and at least one customer — because customers are tuned in to benefits that you may not even consider to be benefits. Example, I have a friend who patronizes a certain bookstore regularly, not because of their books, but because of the carrot cake they serve in their cafe. Once you have a list of your benefits, select your competitive advantage because that's where you'll hang your marketing hat. If you haven't got a competitive advantage, you'll have to create one because you'll need it. After all, anyone can come up with a benefits list. Figure out why people should patronize your business instead of that of a competitor.

3. Step number three is to select the weapons you'll use. In Chapter Three, I listed an even 100 weapons from which

you may make your selection. My recommendation is to use as many weapons as you can. More than fifty of the hundred weapons are free. After you've selected the weaponry, put the weapons into priority order. Next to each weapon, write the name of the person who is in charge of masterminding the use of the weapon plus the date it will be launched. Consider each date you write to be a promise you are making to yourself. Guerrillas do not kid themselves or lie to themselves, so be realistic.

4. The fourth step is to create a guerrilla marketing strategy. The way to do this is elaborated upon in detail in Guerrilla Marketing Chapter Four. I'll let you find it later rather than taking your time right now.

5. Step five is to make a guerrilla marketing calendar. This should be twelve rows long and five columns wide. The first column is called "Month" — listing in which month of the twelve, you did what you did, in marketing. The second column is called "Thrust" — referring to the thrust of your marketing that month. What were you saying? Offering? The third column is called "Media" and it refers to which media you were using that month. The fourth column is called "Cost" and lets you project how much you'll be spending that month. The fifth column is called "Results" so you can give a

letter grade to the month — you know, an A, B, C, D or F. After one year, you compare your calendar to your sales figures and eliminate all but the A's and B's. It takes about three years to get a calendar loaded with slam dunks. Once you have one you'll feel like the client who said of his, "It's a lot like going to heaven without the inconvenience of dying."

6. Step six is to locate fusion marketing partners, businesses with the same prospects and the same standards as you have. Offer to go in on co-marketing ventures with them. Trade links online. Trade lead lists each month. The motto of the millennium: fuse it or lose it.

7. This is the step when you launch your guerrilla marketing attack. The idea of a guerrilla marketing attack is to select a lot of weapons, then launch them in slow motion — at a pace that feels comfortable financially and emotionally. My average client takes 18 months to launch an attack. Don't rush.

8. The eighth step, and this is a toughie, is to maintain the attack. The first seven steps are extremely simple compared to this step. Maintaining the attack means sticking with your plan and your weapons even though you don't get the instant gratification you want so much. Everyone wants success to come instantly, but it doesn't happen that way in real life. The Marlboro Man and Marlboro Country helped make

Marlboro cigarettes the most successfully marketed brand in history. But after the first year of marketing, they didn't increase sales one bit for Marlboro. Maintaining the attack made it happen.

9. Step nine is to keep track. Some of your weapons will hit bull's-eyes. Others will miss the target completely. How will you know which is which? By keeping track. By asking customers where they heard of you. By finding out what made them contact you. Keeping track is not easy, but it is necessary. If you aren't ready to keep track, you aren't ready to launch your attack in the first place.

10. The tenth and final step is to improve in all areas: your message, the marketing weapons you're using, and your results. A guerrilla marketing attack is a never-ending process. But it works every time.

That's it. Ten steps to succeeding with a guerrilla marketing attack. If it sounds easy, reread this lesson. It works, but it's not easy.

GUERRILLA EXERCISE:

Take the first five steps right now. Begin to take the sixth. Then, you'll be prepared for victory when your attack is in full force. Putting your attack into writing with this exercise will give wings to your dreams.

Check each step of the guerrilla marketing attack that you have taken or will take:

_____ I have done the proper research.

_____ I have written a benefits list.

_____ I have selected the marketing weapons I will employ.

_____ I have written my marketing strategy.

_____ I have prepared my marketing calendar.

_____ I have located fusion marketing partners.

_____ I have launched my attack at a comfortable pace.

_____ I am able to maintain my attack.

_____ I am able to keep track of each weapon's effectiveness.

_____ I have improved each facet of my guerrilla marketing attack.

GUERRILLA ACTION STEPS:

A. Review where you put checkmarks on the checklist above and circle the statements at which no check-mark appears. These are the areas that you must focus upon to succeed with your attack. Be aware of them.

B. Decide upon the specific actions that you will take for each statement so as to mount an effective guer-rilla marketing attack. List these in the space provided beneath each statement for which you have circled the number.

C. Take the actions you have listed, one by one, until each of the statements merits a checkmark. Your goal is a checkmark by each statement. An incomplete attack is a recipe for failure.

CHAPTER 7

Guerrilla Marketing: What Marketing Is Not

GUERRILLA MARKETING: WHAT MARKETING IS NOT

Marketing is all contact from anyone in your company with anyone outside of your company. It's a process and not an event.

~By Jay Conrad Levinson

Guerrillas know that marketing is just a fancy word for selling and treating people well. It is more common sense and patience than anything else. But people think marketing is a bunch of things it isn't. Let's look at what marketing is not.

1. Marketing is not advertising. Don't think for a second that because you're advertising, you're marketing. No way. There are over 100 weapons of marketing. Advertising is one of them. But there are 99 others. If you are advertising, you are advertising. You are doing only 1% of what you can do.

2. Marketing is not direct mail. Some companies think they can get all the business they need with direct mail. Mail order firms may be right about this. But most businesses need a plethora of other marketing weapons in order for their direct mail to succeed. If you are doing direct mail only, you're no guerrilla.

3. Marketing is not telemarketing. For business-to-business marketing, few weapons succeed as well as telemarketing — with scripts. Telemarketing response can be dramatically improved by augmenting it with advertising. Yes, advertising, and direct mail. Yes, direct mail. Marketing is not telemarketing — alone.

4. Marketing is not brochures. Many companies rush to produce a brochure about the benefits they offer, then pat themselves on the back for the quality in the brochure. Is that brochure marketing? It is a very important part when mixed with 10 or 15 other very important parts — but all by itself? Forget it.

5. Marketing is not the yellow pages. Most, and I mean most companies in the U.S. run a yellow pages ad and figure that takes care of their marketing. In 5% of the cases, that's the truth. In the other 95%, it's disaster in the form of marketing ignorance. Sure, have a yellow pages ad as part of your arsenal. But only part.

6. Marketing is not show business. There's no business like show business, and that includes marketing. Think of marketing as sell business, as create-a-desire business, as motivation business. But don't think of yourself as being in the entertainment business, because marketing is not supposed to entertain as much as it is to generate honest profits.

7. Marketing is not a stage for humor. If you use humor in your marketing, people will recall your funny joke, but not your compelling offer. If you use humor, it will be funny the first and maybe the second time. After that, it will be grating and will get in the way of what makes marketing work — repetition.

8. Marketing is not an invitation to be clever. If you fall into the cleverness trap it's because, unlike the guerrilla, you don't realize that people remember the most clever part of the marketing even though it's your offer they should remember. Cleverness is a marketing vampire, sucking attention away from your offer.

9. Marketing is not complicated. It becomes complicated for people who fail to grasp the simplicity of marketing, but marketing is user-friendly to guerrillas. They begin with a seven-sentence guerrilla marketing plan, create a marketing calendar, and select from 100 weapons. Not too complicated.

10. Marketing is not having a website. A website may turn out to be your single most valuable marketing weapon, but all by itself, it is not marketing. In fact, it must be marketed with the same energy you use to market your primary offering.

11. Marketing is not a miracle-worker. More money has been wasted due to marketers expecting miracles than to any other misconception of marketing.

Marketing is the best investment in America if you do it right, and doing it right requires commitment, patience and planning. Expect miracles get ulcers.

Before I let you scour the Net for more nuclear-powered gems for your business, I feel honor-bound to let you know that marketing is an opportunity for you to earn profits with your business, a chance to cooperate with other businesses in your community or your industry, and a process of building lasting relationships.

Marketing is a topic that intimidates many business owners, so they steer clear of it. For guerrillas, marketing has no mystique at all and is a whale of a lot of fun because they enjoy launching a marketing attack and knowing they'll succeed. Guerrillas know well what marketing is and they certainly know what marketing is not.

GUERRILLA EXERCISE:

Examine all of your past marketing efforts to determine which ones are real marketing and which ones are not. Begin concentrating on doing more of those which are marketing and eliminate those which are only pretenders.

Put a checkmark next to each marketing truism that characterizes your current marketing:

_____ My marketing is not merely advertising.

_____ My marketing is not merely direct mail.

_____ My marketing is not merely telemarketing.

_____ My marketing is not merely a brochure.

_____ My marketing is not merely a yellow pages listing.

_____ My marketing is not show business.

_____ My marketing is not merely a stage for humor.

_____ My cleverness does not get in the way of my message.

_____ I do not consider marketing too complicated to control.

_____ My marketing is more than merely having a website.

_____ I do not expect miracles from my marketing.

GUERRILLA ACTION STEPS:

A. Circle each truism that does not have a checkmark.

B. List the action you will take, in the space provided, to earn a checkmark for each listed insight into marketing that you possess.

C. Execute your marketing in a way that reflects your insights, profiting by your understanding of what marketing is and is not.

CHAPTER 8

Guerrilla
Marketing Myths

GUERRILLA MARKETING MYTHS

The path to entrepreneurial success is mined with booby traps disguised as words of wisdom. Guerrillas can distinguish the facts from the fables.

~By Jay Conrad Levinson

There are many marketing myths that ought to be tucked away where you keep the collected works of the Brothers Grimm, Aesop and Mother Goose. They may be fun to read, but they are disastrous to any marketing campaign. Heaven help us, there are hundreds of these myths circulating, but we'll deal only with ten of them here because if I wrote about all of them, your computer would probably crash while laughing in disbelief.

Myth:

It's good to have a lot of white space in advertisements, brochures, and other printed material.

Truth:

Your prospects and customers care a whole lot more about information than blank space. They want to know what your offering can do for them, not that you can afford to run a lot of white space. Usually white space substitutes for powerful ideas, a list of benefits and a fertile imagination. Attention should be drawn by substance, not emptiness. Yes, white space is aesthetically pleasing, but profits are even more delightful.

Myth:

Use short copy because people just won't read long copy.

Truth:

People real long books, long articles and long letters. They read whatever interests them, and the more they're interested, the more they'll read. If you give people more data than they need, they'll either buy from you or they won't buy. If you give them less, they won't buy — period. Studies show that readership of marketing materials falls off dramatically after the first 50 words, but stays high from 50 words to 500 words. That means your non-prospects will turn the page in a hurry, but your prospects will read and hang on to every word, trying to learn as much as they can.

Myth:

It is costly to purchase television time.

Truth:

This myth was once the truth, but cable and satellite TV have obliterated it. The cost to run a prime time commercial in any major market in the U.S. is now $20 or less, often as low as $5. Better still, cable TV allows you to cherry-pick where your commercials will run so that they air only in communities where your prospects live. You can advertise on CNN, MTV, ESPN, A&E, The Discovery Channel — any satellite-delivered programming. And cable companies will produce your spot for a cost near $1000, a far cry from the $197,000 average spent on production in 2004.

Myth:

Sell the sizzle, not the steak.

Truth:

The idea is to sell the solution, not the sizzle. The easiest way to sell anything is to position it as the solution to a problem. If you look for the sizzle and not the problem, you're looking in the wrong direction. Your prospects might appreciate the sizzle, but they'll write a check for the solution. Your job is to spot the problem then offer your product or service as the solution. If you think solutions, you'll market solutions. If you think sizzle, you'll sell sizzle. You'll find that the path of least resistance to the sale leads right through the problem to the solution.

Myth:

Truly great marketing works instantly.

Truth:

First-rate sales work instantly. Great limited-time offers work instantly. But great marketing is not made up of sales and limited-time offers alone. These will attract customers, but they won't be loyal and they'll be won by whoever offers the lowest price. Great marketing is made up of creating a desire for your offering in the minds of qualified prospects, then peppering your offers with sales and limited-time offers. But a program of fast-buck marketing usually leads to oblivion. The best marketing in America took a long time to establish itself. Just ask the Marlboro man. Or the Green Giant. Or that lonely Maytag repairman. None of that marketing worked instantly, but it has worked for decades and still does.

Myth:

Marketing should entertain and amuse.

Truth:

Show business should entertain and amuse. But marketing should sell your offering. This widespread myth is based upon studies that show people like marketing that entertains. They like it but they sure don't respond to it. Alas, the marketing community nurtures this myth by presenting awards based upon glitz and glitter, humor and originality, special effects and killer jingles. Those awards should be given for profit increases and nothing else. The only thing that should glitter should be your bottom line.

Myth:

Marketing should be changed regularly to keep it fresh and new.

Truth:

The longer that solid marketing promotes a product or service, the better. Guerrillas create marketing plans that can guide their efforts for five or ten years, even longer. How long have people been in good hands with Allstate? How long have Rice Krispies snapped, crackled and popped? Do you think these marketers would be more successful if they kept changing the marketing around to keep it fresh? I think not.

Myth:

Marketing is successful if it is memorable.

Truth:

Marketing is successful if it moves your product or service at a profit. Memorability has nothing to do with it. Whether people like it or not has nothing to do with it. Studies continue to prove that there is no relationship between remembering your marketing and buying your offering. All that matters is if people are motivated to make a purchase. So don't aim for memorability as much as desirability because that leads to profitability.

Myth:

Bad publicity is better than no publicity at all.

Truth:

Bad publicity is bad for your business. No publicity is a lot healthier for you. People just love to gossip, especially about businesses that have done something so awful that the media exposes it. Guerrillas love publicity but avoid bad publicity because they know it spreads faster than wildfire.

Myth:

All that really counts is earning a honest profit.

Truth:

Good taste and sensitivity also count. Marketing, as part of mass communications, is part of the evolutionary process. It educates, informs, announces, enlightens and influences human behavior. Because it does, it has an obligation to offend nobody, to present its material with taste and decency, to be honest and to benefit customers. If it does that and earns profits too, it is true guerrilla marketing.

GUERRILLA EXERCISE:

Notice the newspaper advertising, magazine ads, television spots, radio commercials direct mail, email, and websites designed to motivate you. Make a list of ten examples of this marketing that arises from people believing in the mythology of marketing. This will help you realize that as a guerrilla, you will never run a mythological marketing campaign.

Make a checkmark by each of the myths that you do not believe:

_____ It is good to have a lot of white space in marketing materials

_____ People do not read long copy.

_____ It is very costly to purchase time on television.

_____ Marketing should sell the sizzle and not the steak.

_____ Good marketing works instantly.

_____ Marketing is supposed to entertain and amuse.

_____ Marketing should change regularly.

_____ Marketing should be memorable above all else.

_____ Bad publicity is better than no publicity.

_____ The only purpose of marketing is to earn a profit.

GUERRILLA ACTION STEPS:

A. Circle each statement that does not have a checkmark.

B. List the action you will take to cease your belief in a myth. Your goal is a checkmark next to each myth.

C. Adjust your current marketing to reflect the truths of marketing and operate by none of the myths.

CHAPTER 9

Guerrilla Marketing With Technology

GUERRILLA MARKETING WITH TECHNOLOGY

The greatest boom to guerrilla marketing has been the inexpensive, powerful and easy-to-use technology of today. I hate saying the word "empower," but technology definitely empowers a small business.

~By Jay Conrad Levinson

Up till a few years ago, technology was not associated with small business marketing. It was connected with databases, inventory control, electronic spreadsheets and word processing. It was complicated, costly — and its affect on small business didn't stretch into the arena of marketing.

But that was then.

Now, technology is in the process of revolutionizing small business, enabling many small business owners to dream new dreams, then attain them in surprisingly brief time spans. Sure, technology helps all businesses in all ways. **But it helps small businesses in the biggest ways**.

For one thing, technology gives small businesses a blatantly **unfair advantage** because it allows them to look and act big without having to spend big. The price of credibility has dropped while credibility itself has become more precious. Technology provides small business owners with **the tickets to credibility** — season tickets — in fact, lifetime tickets.

Until recently, the advantages of small business over big business were gained by utilizing the weapons of personalized service, extra flexibility, and speed. Today, guerrilla business owners, those who want conventional goals using unconventional means, have a secret weapon. That weapon blasts open the doors to increased profits.

The secret weapon is technology — though the secret is getting out as those who know it are unable to hide the grins on their faces. Technology is more simple than ever, so simple that high-tech is becoming easy-tech. It's so inexpensive that in 2005, you can invest a low four figure sum to purchase what in 1982 took a mid six figure sum.

Technology has evened out the playing field, removed the dome from the top and opened the entire world to the entrepreneur. Online, that practitioner of free enterprise can connect with allies and customers anywhere in the community and on the planet. That small business owner has learned that **virtual is a state of mind that means "connected."** Being connected has never been so low in cost and high in value.

To many guerrilla marketers, technology is to be lauded because **it has put them online** — giving them access to the speed of email, the power of fresh information, the warmth of closely connected people, and the marketing muscle of the World Wide Web. To others, technology is the hero because it allows them to flourish in a home-based business.

Examining just those areas where technology adds potency to marketing, I find 20 that are especially intriguing if you take seriously the business of earning consistent profits.

1. The first way is in the area of **marketing online**. A computer can help you design and then post your own website online. But before you rush off and do that, heed this: a website cannot help you **unless you know marketing**. It is a marketing medium, perhaps the best and most comprehensive ever — but it is not marketing all by itself and it is no guarantee of success. You must be an ace marketer in order to market online successfully. You've got to know how to market what you sell as well as marketing your website. **The moment you think of going online is when to start thinking of promoting your website offline.** That process should never stop.

    Marketing online doesn't merely mean the web. It means emailing, posting notices at forums, engaging in chats, doing research, gathering market data **and** having a website. The keys to succeeding online are in creating compelling content, changing that content regularly, responding at nearly the speed of light, and personalizing your messages. There may be 100 million people on the Internet but your prospects must feel you're talking to them one at a time.

I promised you 20 ways that technology helps you market and then I went off on a tangent because I want you to use technology the right way online.

I also want you to be aware of 19 ways technology can help you offline:

2. **Newsletters** — Good ones are mailed to customers and prospects on a regular basis and follow the rule of 75-25.

3. **Flyers** — Distribute them in a variety of ways: as signs, in orders, to fusion marketing partners to distribute as you distribute theirs.

4. **Direct mail letters** —Have an inventory of proven letters in your computer, set to print, personalize and mail.

5. **Postcards** — They take away from the recipient the decision of whether or not to open the envelope.

6. **Business cards** —- Include your name, company name, title, address, phone, fax number, email address, website, logo, theme line; your card may open up to reveal a list of benefits offered and services available.

7. **Brochures** — Perfect forums for including all the details; they should be offered for free in your other marketing and posted online.

8. **Catalogs** — You can increase revenues through catalogs, now easy and inexpensive to design and produce, a potentially big profit-center.

9. **Gift certificates** — People are on the lookout for gift ideas and a gift certificate might be perfect. Mention them on signs, in brochures.

10. **Coupons** — Offer discounts, free merchandise, services, anything to intensify prospect's desire for your product. Coupons are very versatile.

11. **Contest entry forms** — Smart small businesses hold contests in order to get names for their mailing lists.

12. **Club ID cards** —Form a frequent buyer club or VIP customer club: sealing your relationship with the customers with an attractive ID card.

13. **Signs** — Because so many towns have community bulletin boards, guerrillas are sure to post their signs on those boards. Guerrillas know that computers can transform some signs into posters.

14. **Point-of-purchase materials** — Guerrillas produce POP materials that tie in with their other marketing. Their computers do the hard work.

15. **Trade show materials** —You can produce compelling graphic presentations of sales stories strictly for use at trade shows.

16. **Flip charts** — Audio-visual aids are built-in and your sales story has an order and flow. These can be portable, economical, and flexible.

17. **Books** — Technology helps guerrillas from producing labels and tags to self-publishing their own books, proving they're the experts.

18. **Invitations** — Guerrillas print formal invitations to customers to private sales, parties and special events. They always play favorites.

19. **Proposals** — Computer-designed proposals add credibility, visibility, and excitability while instilling confidence in you beyond any price tag.

20. **Multi-media presentations** —These once complex and now simple forums let you demonstrate your benefits with extraordinary impact.

Technology lets small business gain credibility and provide speed and power in an age when credibility is crucial, speed is revered and power comes from being part of a team. Speed comes from cellular, wireless, pager, fax, email, and voicemail technology. Power comes from networking and sharing technology.

If you're guerrilla marketing with technology, you're headed in the right direction. If you're guerrilla marketing without technology, you're not really guerrilla marketing at all.

GUERRILLA EXERCISE:

Make three lists now. The first should contain the technology you are using right now. The second should contain the technology you'll be using within two years. The third should contain the technology that your customers use. The closer the third list is to your first list and second list, the better you are marketing properly with technology.

Put a checkmark next to each of the technologies you currently employ:

_____ Fax machine

_____ Voice mail

_____ Pager

_____ Cell phone

_____ Computer

_____ High speed Internet access

_____ Wireless technology

_____ Two-way radio

_____ CD-ROM

_____ Palm pilot

GUERRILLA ACTION STEPS:

A. Circle each technology your business currently lacks.

B. Determine whether an investment in each technology you are not employing will increase your overall profitability.

C. Write a list of which missing technology you will acquire and the month and year you will acquire it. The goal is to have technology that matches that of your customers and that earns profits for your business.

CHAPTER 10
Guerrilla Tickets To Ride Into The Millennium

GUERRILLA TICKETS TO RIDE INTO THE MILLENNIUM

This is not your father's millennium. This is a whole new ballgame and your tickets to the old ballgame won't get you very good seats.

~By Jay Conrad Levinson

Entering into one millennium from another is a good time to reexamine the baggage you'll be bringing along. In the area of marketing, you'll certainly have to leave behind a lot of old ideas and myths, notions and traditions. But you surely want to take with you at least the five essential tickets to ride into that new millennium with confidence in your success.

Guerrillas enter the new millennium with momentum because they have those tickets. They know exactly where they're heading and they have the right tickets to their destinations. To generate and capitalize upon your own momentum, to travel first-class into the future, it makes sense for you to learn the five destinations of the guerrilla and their five tickets to ride. You can go to the same destinations; you can have the same tickets:

1. The first is your **Identity Ticket**. It's the ticket that leads to close relationships. You get it with consistent and never-ending follow-up. You stay in touch with your customers and key prospects so regularly that you become part of their identity, someone they trust, someone they refer to their friends and associates. You convey your own identity in all of your marketing to them so they know clearly who you are and why you're good. Because you know that marketers either follow-up forever or fail, follow-up is your middle name. I can read it there on your Identity Ticket.

2. The second is your **Humanity Ticket**. Whatever new and brilliant technologies you select to energize your company in the marketing arena, you always remember that your customers and prospects are people first, every one of them unique and special. So your marketing messages to them are warm and human, attentive to details of their lives, caring of their progress, helpful and informative, personalized whenever possible. This ticket leads to bonding and loyalty, far in excess of that enjoyed by most small business owners. Customer research questionnaires provide the information guerrillas need to prove their humanity. It's vital in an increasingly impersonal society.

3. The third is your **History Ticket**. Lots of new and start-up companies, especially those that sprung up after January 1st,

1999, have no histories. You do and your ticket leads to credibility. The more you have, the easier it is to buy from you. Your history ticket is dated from the day you launched your business, includes your marketing strategy, your list of satisfied customers, your past success stories, your past publicity reprints, everything you've done to earn the confidence of your market. That History Ticket, probably presented on your website, in your brochure, in your mailings, in your ads, will bypass the skepticism that faces new businesses and pave the way to future sales with trust.

4. The fourth is your **Technology Ticket**. Of course, you've conquered all traces of technophobia and now use technology to help you serve customers, scout for new prospects, link with fusion marketing partners, research the competition and create a plethora of marketing materials for yourself. This ticket leads to professionalism, but it has side tracks that lead to places you don't really want to go. Many lead to an over-reliance on what technology can do rather than what it can do for you. Some side tracks lead you to glamour and hype instead of useful information, others to glitz and flash that your website visitors don't want to see, still others to fill your TV and print ads with special effects instead of reasons to want what you offer. Guerrillas stay on the right track with their technology, using it as a guide and not as a master.

5. The fifth ticket is your **Action Ticket**. It leads to accomplishment instead of conversation. That ticket is where you find your road map in the form of your marketing calendar. It's where you can see the specific tasks you must perform so as to keep your marketing in constant action, to keep your name at the forefront of your market's awareness. The other tickets are worthless unless your Action Ticket is put to full use. Marketing is something that many people discuss and analyze, but guerrillas view it as a time and opportunity to take action, to do something, to capitalize upon the momentum they've achieved to go soaring into the new millennium, not missing a beat.

These five tickets are yours if you have the awareness of their importance, the desire to reach their destinations, and the attitude to use them with enthusiasm. With that awareness, desire and attitude, you're well-equipped to enter a new century with exactly what you need for profits, control and certainty.

GUERRILLA EXERCISE:

You saw this one coming. Determine which of the five tickets you already hold, then determine which ones you'll need, then do all it takes to get them. Without them, we both know you're in a river and you don't have a paddle.

Place a checkmark next to each of the tickets you already hold:

_____ An Identity Ticket

_____ A Humanity Ticket

_____ A History Ticket

_____ A Technology Ticket

_____ An Action Ticket

GUERRILLA ACTION STEPS:

A. Circle each ticket that does not have a checkmark next to it.

B. State the action you will take to earn this ticket, using the space beneath each ticket.

C. Take each action you have listed so that you hold all five tickets.

CHAPTER 11
The Importance Of Permission

THE IMPORTANCE OF PERMISSION

With so much interruption marketing going on these days, the way to succeed is to gain permission to market to people. Once you have it, you're in clover. Without it, you're in — I-don't-want-to-say-it.

~By Jay Conrad Levinson

Sometimes the student becomes the teacher. That's exactly what happened to me when Seth Godin, co-author of three books with me, authored his own "Permission Marketing: Turning Strangers into Friends and Friends into Customers." It changed my entire outlook about marketing and can dramatically change the beauty of your bottom line.

Seth, once a student of mine, now has enlightened me to the presence of two kinds of marketing in the world today. The first, most common, most expensive, most ineffective and most old-fashioned, is **interruption marketing**.

That's when marketing such as a TV commercial, radio spot, magazine or newspaper ad, telemarketing call, or direct mail letter interrupts whatever you're doing to state its message. Most people pay very little attention to it, now more than ever because there is so much of it and because many minds now unconsciously filter it out.

The opposite of interruption marketing is the newest, least expensive, and most effective kind. It's called **permission marketing** — because prospects give their permission for you to market to them.

It works like this. You offer your prospects an enticement to volunteer to pay attention to your marketing. The enticement may be a prize for playing a game. It could be information prospects consider to be valuable. It might be a discount coupon. Perhaps it's membership to a privileged group such as a frequent buyer club, a birthday club. Maybe it's entry into a sweepstakes. And it might even take the form of an actual free gift. All you ask in return is **permission to market to these people**. Nothing else.

Alas, you'll have to use interruption marketing in order to secure that important permission. And you'll have to track your costs like crazy, figuring how much it costs you to gain each permission — easily figured by analyzing your media costs divided by number of permissions granted.

Once you've embarked upon a permission marketing campaign, you can spend less time marketing to strangers and more time marketing to friends. You can move your marketing from beyond mere reach and frequency and into the realm of trust.

Once you've obtained permission from your prospects, your marketing will take on three exciting characteristics. It will be

anticipated, meaning people will actually look forward to hearing from you. It will be **personal**, meaning the messages are directly related to the prospect. And it will be **relevant**, meaning you know for sure that the marketing is about something in which the prospect is interested.

Permission marketing is not about share of market, not even about share of mind. Instead, it's about **share of wallet**. You find as many new actual customers as you can, then extract the maximum value from each customer. You convert the largest number of prospects into customers, using your invaluable permission to accomplish this. You focus your marketing only on prospects and not on the world at large.

Let's use an existing coed summer camp as an example of permission marketing in action. The camp uses interruption marketing to run ads at camp fairs and in magazines that feature other ads from summer camps. But the ads do not attempt to sell the summer camp. Instead, they focus solely upon motivating prospects to send for a video and a brochure, upon securing their permission to accept your marketing with an open mind.

Once the prospects receive the video, they soon see that it, too, does not try to sell the camp. It is geared only to get permission to set up a meeting. But having seen a video of the camp facilities, activities, happy campers and attentive staff, the prospect is all set to say yes to a personal meeting.

At the in-person meeting, the sale is closed. And once a camper attends the camp for one summer, chances are pretty darned good he or she will not only stay for several more summers, but also will bring along a brother, a sister, a cousin, a schoolmate or a friend — or all of these.

Notice that the only goal of each step is to expand permission for you to take another step rather than making the ultimate sale. Who uses permission marketing these days? Record clubs. Book clubs. Marketers who offer a free brochure. Even my own website at gmarketing.com offers you something free, just for signing up with us — in affect, gaining permission to market to all those who sign up.

The biggest boon to permission marketing is the internet — but only by those who treat it as an interactive medium and not like TV. As clutter becomes worse, permission become more valuable. The moral: since only a limited number of companies within a market niche can secure permission, get moving on your own permission marketing program pronto.

GUERRILLA EXERCISE:

Make a list of the methods you'll use to gain permission, then what marketing materials you'll use once you have that permission.

Make a checkmark next to each marketing weapon you use in order to gain consent to send more marketing materials:

_____ Newspapers

_____ Radio

_____ Television

_____ Magazine ads

_____ Newspaper ads

_____ Direct mail letters

_____ Direct mail postcards

_____ Postcard for postcard deck

_____ Telemarketing

_____ Website

_____ Email

_____ Trade shows

_____ Brochures

_____ Seminars

_____ Yellow pages ads

_____ Classified ads

_____ Movie ads

Now, put a checkmark next to each item you offer in order to broaden your consent:

_____ Brochure

_____ Website

_____ Free consultation

_____ Video

_____ Audio tape

_____ Demonstration

_____ Free estimate

_____ Free gift

_____ Newsletter

_____ Ezine

_____ Catalog

_____ Poster

GUERRILLA ACTION STEPS:

A. Circle each weapon you are not using to gain or broaden consent from your prospects to receive marketing materials.

B. Make a list of the actions you will take to employ each weapon and the month and year you will begin to employ it.

C. Activate each weapon, one by one, so as to gain consent from all of your prospective customers.

CHAPTER 12

Guerrilla Marketing As Sex

GUERRILLA MARKETING AS SEX

If you view marketing as one big and profitable mating ritual, you'll be viewing it in
exactly the right way.

~By Jay Conrad Levinson

The whole idea of guerrilla marketing is to transform cold
prospects into consenting partners. As with superb sex,
marketers shouldn't be in a hurry, shouldn't direct their energies to
disinterested people and must realize that the consummation of a
loving relationship won't take place without proper wooing, without knowing exactly what turns on the prospect.

When small business owners think less of marketing as impersonal communications and more as sexual journey, they will be far
more able to market with success. In today's cluttered environment of marketing, instead of pondering numbers and demo-
graphics, explore instead the concepts of romance and love.

That means realizing that falling in love with the right person
and keeping the relationship delicious and satisfying is not so
much a single major event as a step-by-step process. It begins by
playing the field and determining just who you want to date in the
first place. During this step, guerrilla marketers concentrate upon

the compatibility factor. They keep their radar attuned to the proper chemistry that leads to mutual understanding and eventual consent. Unfazed by superficial allure, they seek soulmates more than customers. Their taste and discretion helps reduce their marketing costs because their targets reflect quality over quantity.

Their next step is gaining uncarnal knowledge. They seek information about prospects who have caught their fancy so they can satisfy their needs more than their wants — because guerrillas realize people often want what they don't need, and providing it is hardly the basis of a long term relationship. They seek shared values in customers as they would in lovers, gaining information as they impart information, much in the manner of two people getting to know each other — with romance on their mind.

They treat all prospects differently, just as they want to be treated. They learn those ways with research and two-way communication.

It's at this point that guerrillas engage in **flirting** — taking that first step towards gaining consent. Marketing with personalized messages, treating advertising not as the way to make the sale but as the first step in gaining consent, they become attractive to those who have attracted them.

When **the courtship begins**, guerrillas pay very close attention and prove that they care. They enter into dialogues with those for whom they are lusting and know what to say for that lust to be returned. Any courtship is intensified with gifts of love, and it is no different in the guerrilla marketer's search for consenting partners. Gifts can be gift-wrapped or come in the form of prizes, memberships in loyalty groups, newsletters, booklets, regular email updates. Each prospect knows that their individuality is recognized.

Next comes **making out**, connecting even closer with prospects by becoming more intimate in marketing. By listening carefully to learn of likes and dislikes, specific problems, guerrillas learn to make promises they can keep. Their penchant for taking action broadens even more the consent for which they strive.

The step in marketing that most relates to **foreplay** is when marketers give to their partners the exact pleasure that they want. They capitalize upon the interactivity afforded by online communications to become a part of their prospect's identities. They customize their messages to each prospect, not only making them feel special but proving their devotion.

Guerrilla marketers and their prospects achieve **consummation** by closing the sale with mutual consent. Rather than having rushed, their timing is impeccable and their fulfillment implies a commitment. The marketer has consistently demonstrated empathy for the partner — with the goal of providing joy and satisfaction. The earth may not tremble, but a lasting bond has been created.

During **the afterglow**, the connection is solidified. This is accomplished with assiduous follow-up — proving in a way that the marketer still respects the prospect in the morning. Statements of warm appreciation are made resulting in prospects who are so delighted they just cannot help but relate their joy to other people they know.

The entire process involves a lot more than a mere sexual dalliance but is the start of a **long and happy marriage**. The devotion of the small business owner is unmistakable because it builds upon details that have been learned, specific tastes of each customer and their shared experience of sale, purchase and use.

The more you view the marketing process as a mating ritual more than an economic ritual, the longer will be your list of consenting and delighted partners.

GUERRILLA EXERCISE:

Make a list of your hottest prospects, no pun intended, then determine at which stage of the courtship process you are with each of them. Then, you'll know what to do next. All lovers are not created equal. Guerrillas have far more sex appeal.

Place a checkmark next to each of the mating rituals that you follow in marketing your business:

_____ Playing the field

_____ Gaining uncarnal knowledge

_____ Flirting

_____ Courtship

_____ Making out

_____ Foreplay

_____ Consummation

_____ Afterglow

_____ Marriage

GUERRILLA ACTION STEPS:

A. Circle each stage of the mating ritual that you do not employ in marketing your business.

B. Make a list of those rituals.

C. Create the marketing materials you do not use so that you are prepared to carry out the entire marketing/mating ritual. A long and happy marriage comes only after you have taken all the steps to make your customer/partner feel romanced and satisfied.

NOTES:

NOTES:

GET THE COMPLETE GUERRILLA ARSENAL!

Guerrilla Marketing for the New Millennium

A complete reworking of Jay Conrad Levinson's guerrilla "manifesto". Learn to think and market like a guerrilla and crush your competitors.

ISBN: 1-933596-07-4   Paperback

ISBN: 1-933596-08-2   eBook

ISBN: 1-933596-09-0   CD Audio

Guerrilla Marketing: Put Your Advertising on Steroids

Jay Conrad Levinson takes the proven concepts of the world's most successful companies, and synthesized them into a new type of marketing that any business can use to make mega-profits. This is Barely Legal... But You Can Still Get Away With It!

ISBN: 1-933596-13-9   Paperback

ISBN: 1-933596-14-7   eBook

ISBN: 1-933596-15-5   CD Audio

Guerrilla Copywriting

60 Profitable Tips in 60 Enlightening Minutes. Jay Conrad Levinson and David Garfinkel join forces to give small business owners, executives and marketing professionals 60 essential tactics, strategies and concepts for producing highly effective marketing messages.

ISBN: 1-933596-20-1   CD Audio

Guerrilla Marketing During Tough Times

Find Out Why Your Business Is Slowing Down. Jay Conrad Levinson shows you exactly why your business is slowing down in tough economic times and exactly what you can do about it.

ISBN: 1-933596-10-4   Paperback

ISBN: 1-933596-11-2   eBook

ISBN: 1-933596-12-0   CD Audio

Guerrilla Marketing 101: Lessons From The Father Of Guerrilla Marketing — DVD/Workbook Bundle

This 4-Volume set contains over 5 hours of business-building secrets personally presented by Jay Conrad Levinson, Father of the Worldwide Guerrilla Marketing Revolution.

ISBN: 1-933596-16-3   Bundle

ISBN: 1-933596-17-1   DVD

ISBN: 1-933596-18-X   Workbook

Guerrilla Marketing 101: Lessons From The Father Of Guerrilla Marketing — Bootlegged

Over 4 hours of Bootlegged, CD Quality Audio, from the GM 101 Set. Never before revealed tactics and insights from the Father of Guerrilla Marketing.

ISBN: 1-933596-30-9   CD Audio

These items are available through bookstores or directly through Morgan James Publishing at http://www.MorganJamesPublishing.com.

GET YOUR FREE GIFT!

Until now, no marketing association in existence could make a business bulletproof. But once again, Jay Conrad Levinson, the most respected marketer in the world, has broken new ground. The Guerrilla Marketing Association is quite literally a blueprint for business immortality.

Receive a **two-month FREE trial membership** in the Guerrilla Marketing Association where Guerrilla Marketing coaches and leading business experts answer your business questions online and during exclusive weekly telephone chats. This $99 value is your gift for investing in *Guerrilla Marketing For The New Millennium.*

Join right now before your competition does
at http://www.Morgan-James.com/gma.

To purchase additional Guerrilla Marketing products by Jay Conrad Levinson, visit the Morgan James Publishing Bookstore at http://www.MorganJamesPublishing.com.